TRIBES of NATIVE AMERICA

Mohawk

edited by Marla Felkins Ryan
and Linda Schmittroth

BLACKBIRCH®
PRESS

THOMSON
★
GALE™

San Diego • Detroit • New York • San Francisco • Cleveland
New Haven, Conn. • Waterville, Maine • London • Munich

THOMSON

GALE

For more information, contact
The Gale Group, Inc.
27500 Drake Rd.
Farmington Hills, MI 48331-3535
Or you can visit our Internet site at http://www.gale.com

Photo credits: Cover Courtesy of Northwestern University Library; cover © National Archives; cover © Photospin; cover © Perry Jasper Photography; cover © Picturequest; cover © Seattle Post-Intelligencer Collection, Museum of History & Industry; cover, pages © Blackbirch Press Archives; cover, pages 8, 11, 14, 20, 24, 29 © Library of Congress; cover, pages 23, 27, 28 © PhotoDisc; page 6 Courtesy of National Aboriginal Achievement Foundation, Canada; pages 5, 14, 25 © Corel; pages 8, 9, 18 © Hulton Archive; page 8 © North Wind Picture Archives; pages 9, 13, 19 © AP/Wide World Photos; pages 7, 10, 12, 15, 17, 18, 20, 22, 26, 30 © Corbis; page 16 © Bettmann/Corbis; page 21 © Western History/Genealogy Department, Denver Public Library

LIBRARY OF CONGRESS CATALOGING-IN-PUBLICATION DATA

Iroquois/Mohawk / Marla Felkins Ryan, book editor ; Linda Schmittroth, book editor.
    p. cm. — (Tribes of Native America)
Includes bibliographical references and index.
Summary: Discusses the history, government, land disputes, economy, daily life and current issues of the Mohawk people.
  ISBN 1-56711-615-9 (hardback : alk. paper)
1. Iroquois Indians—History—Juvenile literature. 2. Iroquois Indians—Social life and customs—Juvenile literature. 3. Mohawk Indians—History—Juvenile literature. 4. Mohawk Indians—Social life and customs—Juvenile literature. [1. Mohawk Indians. 2. Indians of North America.] I. Ryan, Marla Felkins. II. Schmittroth, Linda. III. Series.
E99.I7 I73 2003
974.004'9755—dc21   2002007802

Printed in United States
10 9 8 7 6 5 4 3 2 1

Table of Contents

MOHAWK

Traditional Mohawk Region

Name

Mohawk (pronounced *MO-hawk*). The Mohawk were given their name by the Algonquin people. The name means "eaters of men." It refers to the Mohawk warriors' custom of eating the bodies of conquered warriors to take in their strength. The Mohawk call themselves *Kanien'Kehake*, which means "People of the Flint." The meaning of this phrase is uncertain.

Mohawk Lands

The Mohawk once lived along the St. Lawrence River in Canada and the Mohawk Valley in central New York State. Today, there are Mohawk reservations in central and upstate New York and several reserves in Canada. (Land that is set aside for the use of American Indians is called a reservation; the Canadians call it a reserve.) A small group of Mohawk also lives on a reservation in Oklahoma.

The Mohawk once lived along the St. Lawrence River in Canada (pictured).

What has happened to the population?

In 1755, there were about 640 Mohawk. In a 1990 population count by the U.S. Bureau of the Census, 17,106 people said that they were members of the Mohawk tribe. Another 8,500 or so Mohawk live in Quebec, Canada.

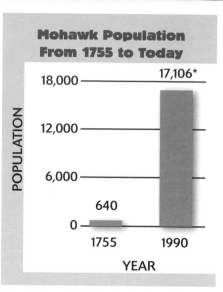

Mohawk Population From 1755 to Today

18,000 — 17,106*

12,000

6,000

640

0

1755   1990

POPULATION

YEAR

*An additional 8,500 live in Quebec, Canada.

Symphony conductor John Kim Bell was born on the Kahnawake Mohawk Reservation near Montreal, Quebec, Canada.

The Mohawk originally lived in longhouses similar this one.

Origins and group ties

The Mohawk descend from people who first lived in what is now the state of New York. They are one of the few American Indian tribes who still live on their original land. The Mohawk are one of the six nations that make up the Iroquois Confederacy. (The others are the Oneida, Onondaga, Cayuga, Seneca, and Tuscarora tribes.) The Mohawk's land straddles the border between New York and Canada.

Mohawk men were fierce fighters who wore the special hairstyle that bears their name. The Mohawk have been at the forefront of the modern native rights movement. They still defy all efforts to weaken their traditional authority and rights.

• Timeline •

1450
The Iroquois Confederacy is founded by Deganawida, "the Peace Maker," and Hiawatha.

1565
Spanish settle St. Augustine, Florida

1607
English colonists settle Jamestown, Virginia

1620
Mayflower lands at Plymouth, Massachusetts

1776
America declares independence from England.

1776
Most Mohawk tribes, led by Thayendanégea, also known as Joseph Brant, side with the British in the Revolutionary War.

HISTORY

Peace and war

The great peacemaker Hiawatha helped found the Iroquois Confederacy. The Iroquois Confederacy brought five (later six) nations that had been at war together in a peaceful, democratic government. Hiawatha may have been a member of the Mohawk tribe, though some experts say he was Onondaga.

Hiawatha is best remembered as the bringer of peace to the warring Iroquois tribes.

The Mohawk traded furs with the French in exchange for European goods. Here, French fur traders travel a river in birchbark canoes.

1861
American Civil War begins

1865
Civil War ends

1917-1918
WWI fought in Europe

1941
Bombing at Pearl Harbor forces United States into WWII

1945
WWII ends

1950s
Reservations no longer controlled by federal government

1989-1990
Debates at Akwesasne Reservation about gambling on the reservation lead to violence

1990
An attempt to build a golf course on Mohawk land in Canada leads to violence

The Mohawk from New York hunted wild game along the St. Lawrence River in Canada. There, they met French traders for the first time in the 1600s. After that, some Mohawk built settlements to be near the French. The Mohawk traded furs to the French in exchange for European goods.

In the 1700s, Europeans came to Mohawk land in present-day New York. They found a large and

A Canadian Mohawk man and boy examine part of a silver communion set given by the English to the Iroquois Confederacy. These pieces went to Canada with the Mohawk during the Revolutionary War.

thriving Mohawk community that the natives called Akwesasne (pronounced ah-kwa-SAHS-nee, which means "where the partridge drums"). Christian missionaries built a mission called St. Regis near Akwesasne in 1752.

When the Revolutionary War began in 1775, there was a bitter split in the centuries-old Iroquois Confederacy. Many Iroquois, especially the Seneca and Onondaga, wanted to stay neutral in the war. The Tuscarora and Oneida, who traded with settlers, fought on the side of the Americans. A Mohawk leader named Thayendanégea convinced some of the Six Nations to fight on the side of the British. The Mohawk at St. Regis chose to support the colonists.

The Iroquois Leagues Confederate Council, which could work only when all six nations agreed, could not come up with a plan of action. Since the tribes did not agree, different nations, villages, and even families had to decide for themselves which side to take. The split in the confederacy never fully healed.

Thayendanégea, who was also known as Joseph Brant, was both an officer in the British army and a

Mohawk war chief. He led troops of Mohawk and British supporters on raids against the colonists' farms and villages. Brant and his fighters also destroyed the food supplies of the colonial armies. When the British lost the war, Brant went with a group of followers to Canada. To reward him for his services in the war, the British gave him a pension and a large piece of land in Ontario, Canada. Many Mohawk and other Iroquois went there, too, and the area came to be called the Six Nations Reserve.

Some groups of Mohawk supported the British during the American Revolution. (pictured). Other Mohawk groups supported the American colonists.

Tribal lands under two governments

After the Revolutionary War, America was independent of the British, but Canada was not. The Mohawk found that their lands were now part of two different countries. This fact still leads to conflicts today.

In 1796, 13 years after Brant fled to Canada, New York State signed a treaty that promised the Mohawk a 36-square-mile (93.2 sq km) reservation. The reservation would include the village of St. Regis and some other lands. Later, New York State

In 1971, Mohawk from the St. Regis Reservation protested against New York legislation that would take some of their land.

The St. Regis Mohawk Reservation (called the Akwesasne Reserve in Canada) stretches from New York State across the St. Lawrence River into Canada.

bought parts of the reservation without the consent it needed from the U.S. government. This led to many land claims. Some of these claims had still not been resolved at the end of the 20th century.

Today, about 10,000 people, both Mohawk and members of other tribes, live at the St. Regis Mohawk Reservation (it is called the Akwesasne Reserve on the Canadian side). The people call themselves the Akwesasne Mohawk tribe. They live on 14,648 acres on the American side and 7,400 acres on the Canadian side. The Mohawk people see themselves as one nation in spite of the boundary drawn through their lands by the United States and Canada.

In 1935, Chief Poking Fire demanded payment from the state of Vermont for hunting grounds taken from the Mohawk many years earlier.

Land claim issues

In recent years, many Native American groups have demanded the return of lands that they claim were taken from them illegally. The Mohawk have long spoken out on these issues.

In 1953, Mohawk Chief Poking Fire sat outside the Vermont State House with about 200 Mohawks. They demanded $1.2 million for the Vermont hunting grounds taken from them 154 years earlier. Then, in 1957, Standing Arrow, a Mohawk, led a group of Indians onto lands claimed

The Mohawk believed that land in the Adirondack Mountains was theirs under a 1784 treaty.

by non-Indians. This land was on Schoharie Creek, near Amsterdam, New York. The Mohawk claimed the land was theirs under a 1784 treaty. To make their point, some Mohawk took over a 612-acre campsite in the Adirondack Mountains for three years. Finally, they reached an agreement with the state of New York in May 1977. The Mohawk were granted two sites within Macomb State Park and near Altoona, New York. The two areas totaled nearly 6,000 acres.

The Mohawk in Canada

The Canadian Mohawk have been just as forceful as the Americans in the fight for their rights. In 1899, 200 Mohawks on the Akwesasne Reserve chased

A Mohawk man
from Canada

away a government police force that tried to make the Indians hold elections. In December 1968, 45 Mohawks from that reserve were arrested as they blocked the bridge from Cornwall, Ontario, to New York. They blocked the bridge to protest Canada's decision to charge them a fee on goods brought from the United States into Canada.

About 8,500 Mohawk live in French-speaking Quebec, Canada. Nearly 1,600 live in and around the small village of Kanesataké (near the town of Oka). Another 6,000 live on the Kahnawake Mohawk Reserve, southwest of Montreal, Quebec's largest city.

Relations between Mohawk residents and the people of Quebec have been tense for many years. This hostility led to violence in 1990. That year, plans were made to enlarge a golf course onto a sacred Mohawk burial site near Oka. In protest, Kanesataké Mohawk set up barriers near the site. When Quebec police tried to take down the barriers, one officer was shot and killed. Police surrounded the Mohawk reserve. At the same time, members of the Mohawk Warrior

Conflicts over Mohawk lands has led to violence.

Society at Kahnawake Reservation blocked a bridge that linked Montreal suburbs to the city. They did this to show their support for the Mohawk at Oka. The action led to a 78-day standoff. The police and the military were on one side and the Mohawk Warriors of Kahnawake and Kanesataké on the other.

White people in Quebec went to the barriers and taunted the Mohawk. The events at Oka were shown each night on news shows. The terrible state of relations between native and non-native Quebec residents shocked many people. The government later bought the disputed piece of land, but there is still some tension.

Government

Today, Mohawk chiefs make up what is known as the Mohawk Nation Council. Supporters view this council as the governing body of the Mohawk people. The council oversees the community as a whole, in both Canada and the United States.

Some officials in Canada, the United States, and New York State think that their agencies and governments should be able to help run the Mohawk Nation. This has led to conflicts. In 1990, for example, two people were killed in arguments over whether there should be gambling on tribal lands.

Former Commissioner of Indian Affairs Louis Bruce grew up on the St. Regis Reservation.

Rosa Minoka Hill, a Mohawk who lived in Wisconsin, was the second Native American woman to become a medical doctor.

A St. Regis Mohawk woman weaves baskets.

Economy

When the French came to what is now Canada in the 1600s, they mainly wanted furs. Mohawk men served as scouts for the French, and searched out the best hunting lands. Other Mohawk men were fur traders and canoe guides. Through trade with Europeans, Mohawk women became world-famous for their woven sweetgrass baskets. In the 1800s, some Mohawk men found work in lumber camps, while others kept their traditional jobs.

At the end of the twentieth century, some of the Mohawk who still lived on reservations worked in a tribe-owned shopping center. Some worked in other businesses, such as construction and tourism. The Mohawk have opened arts and crafts galleries. They let people who are interested in Native American life come to see their celebrations. Like many other tribes, the Mohawk also use gambling as a source of income.

The Akwesasne Mohawk Casino, located on the St. Regis Reservation in New York, provides income to the Mohawk.

DAILY LIFE

Education

In the late 1800s and early 1900s, parents of Indian children across the country were encouraged to send their children to government-run boarding schools. In these schools, students were forbidden to speak their native language or follow their customs. Local public schools also failed to meet Indian needs. By 1968, the Mohawk student dropout rate was an astonishing 80 percent. Mohawk parents demanded that authorities look into why schools failed their children. They became active in education reform.

A classroom in a boarding school for Native Americans in the 1800s

A young Mohawk takes part in a traditional dance in Montreal, Canada.

SOME MOHAWK EXPRESSIONS

shé:kon (SHAY kohn) . . . . "hello"
kwé kwé (KWAY KWAY) . . . . "hello"
hén (hun) . . . . "yes"
iáh (yah) . . . . "no"
niá:wen (nee-AH wun) . . . . "thank you"

Twenty years later, the dropout rate had fallen to below 10 percent.

In 1985, the Akwesasne Mohawk Board of Education was formed on the reservation. Today, it oversees three elementary schools. Some children go to the Akwesasne Freedom School in New York. This school keeps Mohawk culture and language alive for children from preschool through eighth grade. The Mohawk Nation also runs the Native North American Travelling College, founded in 1968. It travels through Canada and the United States to promote Mohawk/Iroquois culture and traditions.

Clothing

Mohawk men were well known for their haircut, which today is called a "Mohawk." One or both sides of the head were shaved to leave a central strip of hair. This strip ran from the

An Iroquois man with a Mohawk hairstyle

A Mohawk child poses with a traditional fur headdress and painted face.

forehead over the top of the head to the back of the neck.

Mohawk people smeared their hair and bodies with grease to protect themselves from insect bites. Men painted their faces blue to show health and well-being, black for war or mourning, and red for either life or violent death.

Arts

The Mohawk skillfully painted and carved wooden objects, such as the cradleboards that they used to carry babies. Some Mohawk women still weave baskets from sweetgrass.

The Mohawk Nation at Akwesasne became one of only about two dozen native communities to own and run a radio station. A magazine called *Akwesasne Notes* and a newspaper are published on the reservation. They help keep the culture alive.

The Mohawk were known for their beautifully carved wooden cradleboards. Cradleboards were used to carry babies.

THE RABBIT DANCE

Mohawk stories often stressed that people should give thanks to the creatures and elements of the world that gave the Mohawk so much. This is an example of such a story.

The rabbit was one of the many animals the Mohawk hunted for food.

Long ago, a group of hunters were out looking for game. They had seen no sign of animals, but they went slowly and carefully through the forest, knowing that at any moment they might find something. Just ahead of them was a clearing. The leader of the hunters held up his hand for the others to pause. He thought he had seen something. All of the men dropped down on their stomachs and crept up to the clearing's edge to see what they could see. What they saw amazed them. There, in the center of the clearing, was the biggest rabbit any of them had ever seen. It seemed to be a big as a small bear!

One of the hunters slowly began to raise his bow. A rabbit as large as that one would be food enough for the whole village. But the leader of the men held out his hand and made a small motion that the man with the bow understood. He lowered his weapon. Something unusual was

(continued) ➡

happening. It was best to just watch and see what would happen next.

The rabbit lifted its head and looked toward the men. Even though they were well hidden on the other side of the clearing, it seemed as if that giant rabbit could see them. But the rabbit did not take flight. Instead, it just nodded its head. Then it lifted one of its feet and thumped the ground. As soon as it did so, other rabbits began to come into the clearing. They came from all directions and, like their chief, they paid no attention to the hunters.

Now the big rabbit began to thump its foot against the

The Mohawk were excellent hunters of game.

ground in a different way. Ba-pum, ba-pum, pa-pum, pa-pum. It was like the sound of a drum beating. The rabbits all around made a big circle and began to dance. They danced and danced. They danced in couples and moved in and out and back and forth. It was a very good dance that the rabbits did. The hunters who were watching found themselves tapping the earth with their hands in the same beat as the big rabbit's foot.

Then, suddenly, the big rabbit stopped thumping the earth. All of the rabbits stopped dancing. BA-BUM! The chief of the rabbits thumped

The thick forests of the Northeast provided many plants and animals that the Mohawk used to survive.

the earth one final time. It leaped high into the air, right over the men's heads, and it was gone. All the other rabbits ran in every direction out of the clearing and they were gone, too.

The men were astonished at what they had seen. None of them had ever seen anything at all like this. None of them had ever heard or seen such a dance. It was all they could talk about as they went back to the village. All thought of hunting was now gone from their minds.

When they reached the village, they went straight to the longhouse where the head of the Clan Mothers lived. She was a very wise woman and knew a great deal about the

(continued) ➡

Iroquois hunters were experts with their weapons.

"Play that rhythm which the Rabbit Chief played," she said.

The leader of the men did as she asked. He played the rhythm of the rabbits' dance.

"That is a good sound," said the Clan Mother. "Now show me the dance which the Rabbit People showed you."

The hunters then did the dance while their leader played the drum. The Clan Mother listened closely and watched. When they were done, she smiled at them.

"I understand what has happened," she said. "The

animals. They told her their story. She listened closely. When they were done telling the story, she picked up a water drum and handed it to the leader of the hunters.

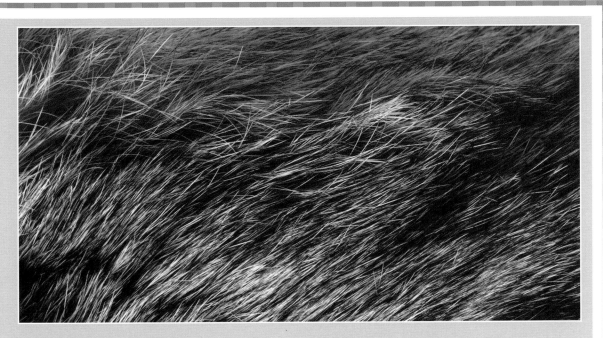

The Mohawk made clothing from rabbit pelts.

Rabbit People know that we rely on them. We hunt them for food and for clothing. The Rabbit Chief has given us this special dance so that we can honor his people for all that they give to the human beings. If we play their song and do their dance, then they will know we are grateful for all they continue to give us. We must call this new song The Rabbit Dance and we must do it, men and women together, to honor the Rabbit People."

So it was that a new social dance was given to the Iroquois people. To this day the Rabbit Dance is done to thank the Rabbit People for all they have given, not only food and clothing, but also a fine dance that makes the people glad.

SOURCE: "The Rabbit Dance." Joseph Bruchac. Native American Animal Stories. Golden, CO: Fulcrum Publishing, 1992.

Hazardous waste is one of the environmental issues that threaten the health and traditional lifestyle of the Mohawk.

Current tribal issues

Along with land claims, environmental issues are a big concern for the Mohawk. The Canadian Mohawk did not want a golf course built on their lands because golf courses use fertilizers and pesticides. The Mohawk think these things are not good for nature. The Mohawk have faced air pollution, contaminated fish, and hazardous waste centers. These things have harmed their health and their way of life. Both the Mohawk and non-native governments have begun to study and deal with these issues.

Notable people

Joseph Brant, also known as Thayendanégea
("He Places Two Bets"), was a Mohawk war chief.
As an officer of the British army, he led Indian
troops in the Revolutionary War (1775-1783).

Joseph Brant, also
known as
Thayendanégea,
was a noted
Mohawk leader.

Jay Silverheels (right), a Mohawk actor, portrayed Tonto, the partner of the Lone Ranger in the hit 1950s television series.

He held talks with both the Canadian and American governments for the land rights of his people. He is said to have translated the Bible into the Mohawk language.

Jay Silverheels (1912-1980) is best known for his role as Tonto, the partner of the Lone Ranger, in a popular television series of the 1950s. Silverheels, whose real name was Harold J. Smith, first came to the United States in 1938. A short time later, he began to act in films. In 1950, he played Geronimo in the movie *Broken Arrow*. This film was one of the first to show Indians in a positive light.

Kateri Tekakwitha (1656-1680) was the first American Indian nun. She was said to have performed many miracles. The Catholic Church chose her in 1980 as a candidate for sainthood.

This statue depicts Kateri Tekakwitha, a Mohawk native. She was the first American Indian nun, and was chosen as a candidate for sainthood by the Catholic Church in 1980.

For More Information

Ballantine, Betty, and Ian Ballantine, eds. *The Native Americans: An Illustrated History.* Atlanta, Georgia: Turner Publishing, 1993.

Bruchac, Joseph. "Otstango: A Mohawk Village in 1491," *National Geographic,* Vol. 180, No. 4, October 1991, pp. 68-83.

Came, Barry. "A Time for Healing: Emotions Still Divide Oka and Kahnawake," *Macleans.* November 12, 1990, vol. 103, no. 46, p. 26.

Mander, Jerry. "Our Founding Mothers and Fathers, the Iroquois," *In the Absence of the Sacred: The Failure of Technology and the Survival of the Indian Nations,* Sierra Club Books, 1991.

Mohawk Nation Council of Chiefs Home Page [http://www.slic.com/~mohawkna/]

Glossary

Confederacy a group of people who join together for a common action or cause

Democratic favoring social equality

Flint a material used for producing a spark;

Neutral a central position—not on any particular side of an issue

Pesticide a chemical used to kill bugs and other pests

Sweetgrass a winter, hardy, sweet smelling grass that grows in rich, moist soil—used to weave baskets

Treaty an agreement

Index